ROSEWOOD AVE.

a poetic journey through love and loss

MARQUAVIOUS MOORE

First published by Marquavious Moore 2024

to A & K

Contents

Love is like a virus.

It can happen to anybody at any time.

— Maya Angelou

ROSEWOOD AVE.

"A Brief Interaction"

Hey!

Hi.

Can I ask you a question?

Sure.

What does *deep emotional intimacy* look like to you?

Bye.

"I Miss You Already?!"

It was three.
We ate.
Life was still for a moment.

There were no desperate attempts
to escape
the vortex that is
catching feelings.
In fact,
we never truly wished
to be free.

Just free enough to remember:
1.) We're just friends.
2.) We're just fucking.
3.) Rome wasn't built in a day...
    (neither was Memphis)

I blame the liquor
for my emotions
I blame the weed
for overthinking
I blame you
for being so goddamn
irresistible.

To be honest,
I blame myself
for realizing
we were
much more than just friends.

You became my favorite person.
You became my favorite excuse
to listen
to the muses
who spoke of vulerability
peeking its head around the corner
as a sprinkle
sets the stage
for an emerging rainbow.

I miss you... already.

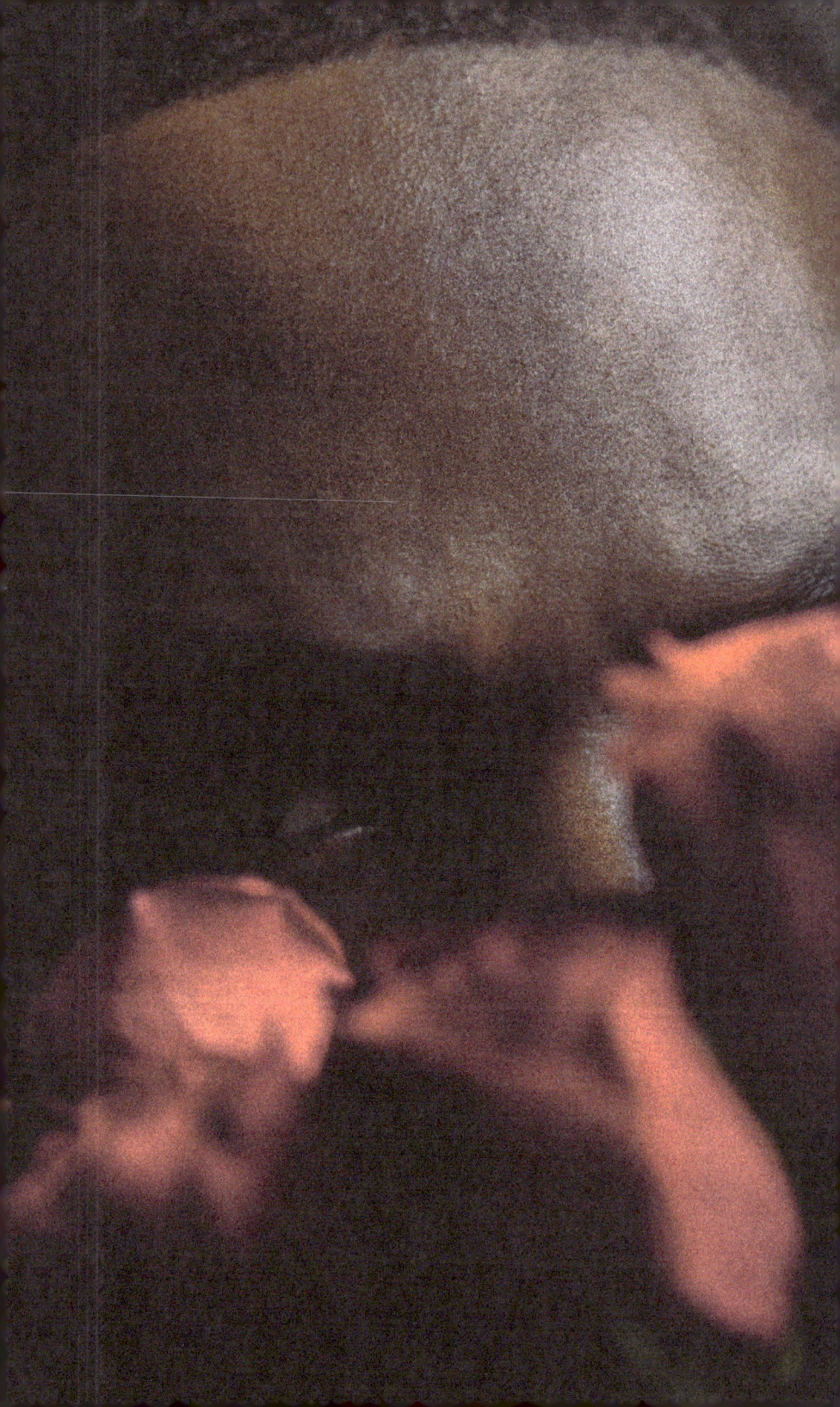

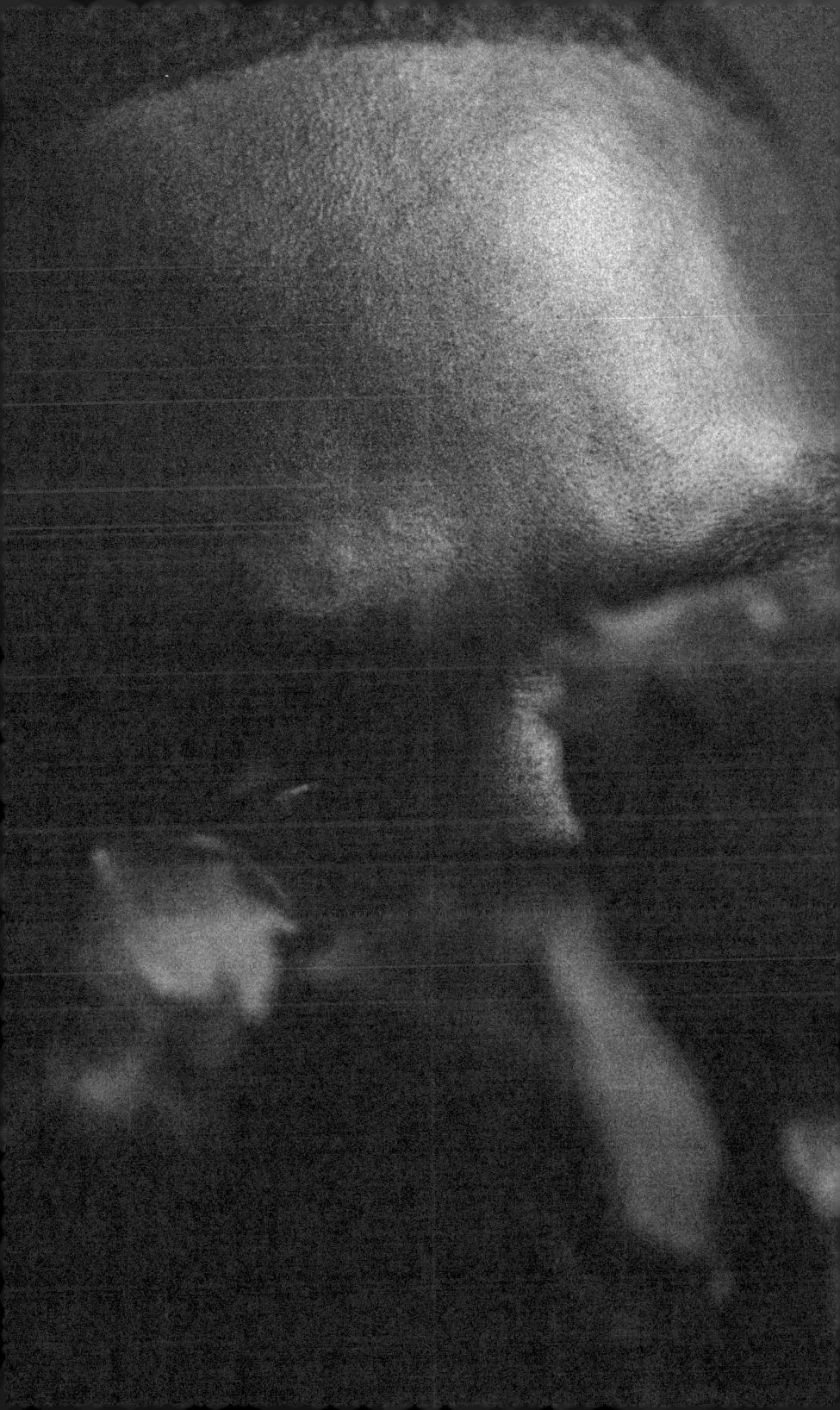

"The Sirens Sing of Karma"

I never understood
the power
of the sirens
until I met you.
Tina warned us
of *A Fool in Love*,
and like the fool
you lured me
to a familiar place.
One of flowers & ash
& gold plated-brass.

Exalted love or exhausted love?

Your love reminds me
of our mortality.
Wanting this to last.
Knowing it won't.

In these times,
I talk
to my ego
and ask
stupid questions like:

Who you fucking when you not with me?
&
How can you fuck someone that isn't me?
&
Am I really that nigga?

I AM. . .

walking on egg shells
knowing that
to be the perfect nigga
is toxic
because nobody's perfect.
Although, goddamit
you're worth the attempt.
You're worth the strain.
But, are you worth my sanity?

I want to feel
the abundance of love.
I want to see
just how much you care.
& I want to know
that *that's* enough.

In these moments,
the ever-fleeting ones,
I'm reminded
of the seasons.
So the sirens,
alluring as they be,
will meet their fate.

"Poems on the Wall"

I'm too busy writing
poems on the wall
to see that
you were the only thing
saving me
from inevitability.

Being inevitably blue —

Cyan,
Sapphire,
Cerulean, too.

Too busy writing
poems on the wall
to ask, "What's your favorite flower?"
Could it be a bouquet of three?
Made of you and me,
& this poem
that won't leave my soul
because the warmth
of your perfume
does a little more than just linger.
It permeates.

Too busy writing
poems on the wall
because these words
reveal the paradox that is
coming too close to saying
I love you,
but not nearly close enough
to what feels like
an the other worldly dance in my soul..

ROSEWOOD AVE.

This feeling should be remembered as fine art:

Timeless;

Tasteful;

Therapeutic, even.

I write these poems on the wall in honor of us,
my dear.

"The Sweetest Treat"

I didn't believe in love.
I never thought it could be,
but how do I explain
the tear-stained
pillow cases
lying underneath me?

I couldn't believe in love.
"A fairy tale for fools."
Well, fairy tales taught us
how to dream,
and you were awakening
more in me than you knew.

How could I not believe in love?
Or explain how I truly feel?
Is it the fear
that holds me back?
Or the fact that I haven't fully healed?

I must believe in love
because you're always on my mind.
I think of you all day
regardless of the time.
*(I wonder if you ate and
when I can eat, too.
Remembering that
the sweetest treat
will always be you.)*

ROSEWOOD AVE.

I believe in love.
I know it exists.
I just never knew it would feel like this.

"Delusional"

I find myself
dancing in a cloud
of disillusionment,
drifting in a sea
of mystery,
learning to trust
the complexity
that is your heart.

Tell me,
do you live in delusion, too?

I find myself
thinking of you
as I ride down
Santa Monica,
questioning everything
you said that
makes me wonder
if you live in delusion, too.

I believe
I like you
enough
to contemplate
whether
the stars are aligning
or if I'm
being blinded by
frivolous fleeting feelings.

I believe
I love you
just enough
to hold
the memory of you closely
because the reality
of not getting
the chance to
hold the real you
seems unforgivable.

*If this is delusional
then I don't care for the truth.
Am I standing in delusion,
& will you stand in it too?*

"Dare Not"

When you talk to your therapist about me, I hope it's all good things. Not how I trigger your PTSD, but that you heal the old versions of yourself through this new relationship with me.

I've never been so seen
which terrifies me
& I've never felt so loved
which comforts me.
*(Your actions show it
though you dare not utter the word.)*

Reality may bring a sobering harshness
so let's cherish the drives through Inglewood,
pass up a few Dons,
and realize that the best view has always been
me with you.

"Pictures of the Moon"

Why do we take pictures of the moon
when we know that
no lens,
or filter,
could ever get it right?

Time and time again,
the photo falls flat,
reminding us that
the best way
to capture anything is
to be present.
To truly witness it.
But, we take them anyway.

So how do I capture your heart?
With my eyes wide open.
Scared that if I blink
I'd miss out on the ecliptic love
right before me.
In time,
the moon will phase,
and so will
this moment.

And there I'll be,
holding on to a memory
that doesn't quite feel right,
that doesn't do the moment justice,
that never tells the full story.

Taking pictures of the moon
reminds me that
the most precious
things in life can't be captured,
just experienced.

So here I am,
holding on to a promising picture,
foreknowing
that though the moon has its phases,
she'll show her cratered backside
once again,
and I'll be waiting
to experience all of this over again, too.

"[i would rather give u flowers]"
inspired by E. E. Cummings

flowers are
perfect[i know u'd love'em] and when
u decide to love something else
i can just buy more flowers
flowers are easy[i only want ur smile]

flowers are
convenient, when u get bored with'em,
throw'em away[ignore'em, forget'em]
curse'em when the petals start to fall and
the fruit flies have taken over ur life

flowers are
cute for the moment[then they're not]
u love'em
for a moment[then u don't]unlike our love
i expect'em to die

[i would rather give u flowers]
because
i can't trust u with my heart
after all, flowers wilt
and so did this[so did we]

"Marigolds and Fire Lilies"

Take a deep breath...
Hold it for a moment...
Now, release.

Let's be
light as a kiss,
light as a breeze,
light as a fallen leaf.

Inhale. Hold. Release.

When past pain put
pity in your heart
the first way to start again
can be by letting go.

Inhale. Hold. Release.

So choose you
when loneliness seek to attack.
Then, look to the moon
and know that I'm looking, too.

For
Love is **now.**
Love is **work.**
Love is **divine.**

Love is choosing
marigolds and marriage
over madness made
by altered memories.

Love is choosing
fucking and fire lilies
over frustrated feelings formed
when lower chakras were set ablaze.

Love is:
The Inhale. The Hold. The Release.

To quiet the mind
can be a difficult hill,
like when G*d hangs up and
you're not done complaining yet.

To quiet the soul?
A testament of will.
Like when you could cry
enough tears it would wash away wars.

Take a moment.
Lean into it.
The Inhale. The Hold. The Release.

Inhale, Hold, Release,
Because somewhere in between
There's peace.

"Juice"

I came in my sleep last night.
I dreamt of being choked,
and long, deep strokes.
Our safe word played on repeat,
though muted and muffled.
I longed for
your toes in my mouth.
From your sole to your soul
I still want all of you.

Now, I sit and think of the times
we had *that* playlist on repeat.
I reminisce of the times
I had your ass in
the palm of my hands,
fueling my God complex.
My ego was the reason
I stared you down
as I licked your cum
off of my fingertips.

I didn't realize
I was getting addicted to you.
I didn't realize
just how addicting it was
laying down with you
and the moon,
and rising
with the sun
as she showcased
her orange lace panties.

27

The way we fucked felt like *agape*,
or whatever love language that was
because in that moment
I felt no shame &
your *agave* dripped off of my lips
as we kissed,
promising how
no amount of seed or soil
could outgrow the love
we had planted in one another.

I came in my sleep last night.
It was the third time this week.
People say
good things cum in three,
but there I was
once again,
sitting in the mess
I had created.
Not quite satisfied.
Alone.

"I Miss You FR"

I miss you
is an understatement
so I smoke L's
on the fire escape,
listening to
a white man
play some of
the jazziest shit ever.

I wonder how we got here?

I miss you
is the diagnosis
I give to wanting
to see
your name
light up
my phone again.
I don't care
that we
swam in survival.

I miss you
is hidden
in the embrace of another.
Distorted is
its reflection
so I escape
to my dreams
instead of wondering
of the intimacies
you share without me.

I miss you
though the trauma
was hidden in the poetry
we held in one another.

I miss you.
I won't stop
missing you
until I start to dream of
butterflies
whose wet wings
gleam as
life gives new love
a fighting chance.

"Dancin' and Dreamin'"

Call me
when you start to dream
so we can
keep this thang goin'
in the astral world.

Let's fantasize about
the time we stopped
to smell
the butterfly lavender.
I still pick them in my dreams.
I don't care
that they're weeds,
and perhaps,
that's the reason
I still dream of you, too.

Dreamin of dancin'
with you never gets old.
Those feet are better, anyway.
Not quite touchin' the ground —
floatin'.

Still,
our paths have done
a lot more than cross,
and perhaps,
that's the reason
I still dream of dancin' with you.

I wonder if you're dreamin' of me, too.
Whether you think
of the songs
we'd do our two-step to,
or if that rain track
does more than just help you
fall asleep.
Perhaps it takes you to
God's personal symphony
in the sky.

Perhaps, perhaps, perhaps...

Call me
when you start to dream,
and don't forget your dancin' shoes.
I'll keep mine on
just in case you decide
to doze off soon.

33

"Cheat Day"

My cheat days often start with
thoughts of you, sex & shrooms.
Everything that
reminds me of the both of us
because what a dream that was.

My cheat days include
texts to my fav just
to say
"I believe in magic"
even though I don't know
if that's fully true.
I'm constantly reminded
that the magic's in the moments
where you

                                      mourn & move on,
                                      mourn & move on,
                                      mourn & move on.

Cheat days make me wonder
why some songs don't hit
the same anymore
while others start to scream
louder than ever.
They remind me that
life is tragic,
and like love,
it must exist with some lost.

On cheat days,
I tell myself,
"small doses."

I have to remember
to give myself grace &
to take deep breaths
because they feel like
little hugs I give my soul.

Cheat days remind me
that I wear my heart on my sleeve
even though it feels
tucked away in my sock.

They remind me to feel
whether it hurts or not.

They help me admit that ultimately
you were just a poem... and that's okay.

"Truth Be Told From A Lying A$$ Nigga"

The memory of you
looking at me like that
lets the flood in.

Tears cascade.

I knew that the damage was done,
but the memory of us
dancing under the moonlight
came rushing in, too.
You still got me.

Cue second set of cascading tears.

Now,
it seems like
the time is best spent
evading a dreadful farewell.
So, we dance.
Skin to skin,
we fit into each other like
the perfect puzzle pieces.

We held on
to each other
as if our hearts depended on it.
We knew that they didn't.
We knew that this was
never meant to last...
but can't we all dream?
(And don't some dreams come true if you work really hard?)

I'm learning
through the tears
just how clear it was that
you loved me.
I just wanted to hear it.

Now, I just want to smell my favorite scent,
again.
That scent being you.
Of course I still crave *that*.
Something **sweeter** than honeydew,
fresher than the morning dew,
and if I'm being honest
cozier than that one perfume
that reminds me of grandma.

We didn't notice how wealthy we were,
but made sure to ignore how poor.
Now I cry in Ubers,
listening to André's new shit,
knowing you'd love it,
wishing you'd just
text me back.
Believe me.
I'm not your enemy.

I know I have to give you space.
I can feel how each text pushes you further and further
away...
But I'm watching the clock.

I know I have to let time do its thing.
But, tick tock.
Tick fucking tock.

I know that I have
to be honest with myself
and admit that I am
actually,
knowingly,
completely,
engulfed in love,
and I am terrified.

Cue final set of tears.
The cascade stops.
The tears remain perfectly still.
Perfectly placed.
Picturesque.

"Sacred Thoughts on the Square"

i'm
thinking
of the day
it started as
hey
& you were
nothing
more than
a stranger
now
i spend
my nights
trapped
in my bed
head full
of desires
to be comforted
in the physical sense
but
oh well
the terrific tale
of how
we were never meant to be
learning that
true power
lies
in vulnerability
questioning
the real reason
i'll never

let you see me cry
call it
ego or pride
a part of me
dies
when you walk away
why can't i ask you
to stay
& still crave you
with such fiendom
knowing
you can't
give me what i need
i still wonder
of what you
dream
ignoring all opportunities
to leave
because
my dog lies at the door
waiting to smell
your scent again
& i sit
waiting too
waiting feels like
dying on the hill
of
indifferent feelings
harboring
the tides of
ill-will
the pedestal
is a bit
dusty
from here
i can see

just how
we were never meant to be
& you can't give me what i need
& i'm sad at
the potentiality
of
what could be
between
you and me

"Our Deepest Fear"
Inspired by Marianne Williamson

Our deepest fear
is not that
we are inadequate.
Our deepest fear
is that
the weeping endures
for more than the night.
Oh, how I've cried 'til morning came, too.

Our deepest fear
is that
all of this
was in vain.
Not knowing whether
we're stuck in a cycle
or enduring the pain
just to realize:
Time doesn't heal shit.
I mean,
look at this!
Look at this mess!
& Who has to put it back together?
Our deepest fear is putting it back together.

Your deepest fear
is divine work
because God,
himself,
seems to be the only one

strong enough
to make me leave you
& God, herself,
must be the only one
that can heal me
when I'm gone.

My deepest fear
is being gone
and something happening to you,
or you being gone
and something happening to me.

How can it be
that our fears rest
somewhere between
getting lost in a hug
and never wanting
to see each other again.
Fearful of the final farewell.

That's it!
Our deepest fear was the
farewell —
the goodbye..

And with goodbye:
the weeping endures;
you put the pieces back together because you have to;
& God comforts me like the baby I am.

"Man in Blue"

Call the cops on the Man in Blue!
Using his male privilege
as niggas do
to walk the streets at night,
searching for 11 or 38
on anything he can find
cuz it was your favorite... allegedly.
He was your favorite... allegedly.

Keep your eye on the Man in Blue!
How he wanted to pull up on you
so many times
just to lay in yo bed
cuz he misses you...
and he still got the code, nigga.
He wants you to trust him,
and he wants to trust you too.

Damn, that Man in Blue.
I swear
the whole neighborhood
gonna know this album
when he through
singing Summer's songs
remixed with sniffles of
a heartbreak that's new.

A heartache so true
he can't help but
miss that type of affection.
Who knows what he'll do
holding on to this kind of rejection?
SO BEWARE!
Here's what you do:
stay guarded and
look out for
the Man in Blue.

"Smell the Roses"

I wanna keep smelling the roses
but the blood has started to drip
& it's beginning to leave a trail

I wipe away my tears
in the middle of the street
cuz I don't want
the neighbors thinkin'
I'm trying to rob 'em

Fuck them
Fuck these tears
& fuck that nigga
that couldn't even tell me he loved me

I want that
which reminds me
how love
is harrowing
humbling
healing

I need to
smell the roses
they remind me that
even the most beautiful things
can hurt, too

They remind me that
I'm good
& good I will remain
even without you

"In Adam"

Inspired by Lauryn Hill

BANG!
BANG!!
BANG!!!
...sounds of
total chaos(total bliss).
Peace is a facade that lives in ignorance.

They shootin',
They shootin',
They shootin' outside while we fuckin'.
They shootin',
They shootin',
They shootin' outside...

Here's to the soular actors;
Fantasy-filled factors;
Rooted in deception
and upheld by hidden masters.
It's not your fault that you can't see the disguise.
With so many distractions,
comes the blinded
and calcified.

They say,
we perish from
the lack of knowledge,
but some things
you shouldn't trust.
Like telling us to pray to
ancestors who
remain anonymous.

Can't you tell?
That you're already in hell?
Put your soul back
on the shelf
because it ain't up for sell.

One day
you'll recognize
how it was you.
Pontius, too.
Looking for the tree
while holding the fruit.
Following the ghosts of empty pursuits.
Lying to yourself like you're
"Obtaining the truth."

Oh, to be a fool!
The mind'll
make you think that
home is a place of solitude.
(I guess God was a poet, too.)

Tail in your mouth,
you're chasing dissatisfaction.
Reality becomes pitiful living out
preconceived infractions.
Be about that action!
Blind leading the blind
can't separate Babylon from Zion.
Scary how living out
"in God we trust"
becomes a government transaction.

Our collective level of morality
is failing us.
Pre-political posts
on Twitter is what
cancelled us.
Congratulations!

You're finally faintly famous.
Finally leaped into lameness.
Following trends
that'll never sustain us,
but can you blame us?
See, freedom
is recognizing
the godliness in the dust
we're made of.
So, lets settle.
Let the dust
in your soul settle
and remember:

It's a lie.
I'm realizing
in Adam I fly.

It's a lie.
I'm realizing
in Adam I fly.

It's a lie.
I'm realizing
in Adam I fly.

"Blessings"

God bless that falling in love shit.
God bless the rise
& the fall of all of it.

God bless you.
I wonder
how life would have been,
to meet you then,
to know the version
of you
before you
believed you
were too hard to love.

God bless you
for choosing you.
For doing what you
were created to do.
All rubied & jaded.

Remember,
under every stone
lies remnants
of an unruly will.
One daring to love
but too scared to.
Claiming not to want
a relationship,
while doing what lovers do.

ROSEWOOD AVE.
God bless me
for loving you anyway —
And cheers to
slow dancing alone in a dark room
while the memory
of your
embrace emits
a warmth so
delicate,
I can only hold onto it
in my dreams.

God bless us.
God bless what was
& what could never be.

And praise be to those who move the fuck on...
Amen.

About the Author

Marquavious Moore is a fresh voice in the publishing world. His poetic journey led him to claim the title of Tennessee's Poetry Out Loud Champion while garnering recognition by the National Civil Rights Museum for his poignant rhymes.

With 'Rosewood Ave.,' his debut self-published poetry collection, Moore invites readers on a journey of self-discovery and profound emotion through his powerful words.

Connect with me online:

Website: www.MarquaviousMoore.com
Instagram: @MDMoore_
Twitter: @MDMoore_